MEET THE PIDDLETONS: IN LOCKDOWN

MEET THE PIDDLETONS: IN LOCKDOWN

By Andrew Robinson

ISBN: 9798675994137 (Paperback)

Front cover image by: Neil Roberts of Nicw Illustrations

First printing edition 2020

Instagram: @andrewrobinsonwriter
Twitter: @AndrewRWriter

Dedication:

To provide some light-hearted comedy to the human population who went through the global pandemic of 2020.

LOCKDOWN WEEKS:

MEET THE PIDDLETONS:

MEET THE PIDDLETONS:

Due to a global pandemic, planet Earth has closed its doors on over 7.5 billion people. A new virus called COVID-19 has started to spread around the world. The Piddletons — that's Daddy, Mummy and two squabbling daughters — are locked down within the confines of their mid-terrace house.

The government brought in drastic measures that sent most human beings home from nurseries, schools and workplaces. Daddy and Mummy are delighted. The daughters think they might be.

People are only permitted outside their house for a daily hop, skip and jump to the shops. They call it a *lockdown*. But it's not a *true* lockdown.

In China, people aren't allowed out of their house without written permission from their leaders and the head of the military.

In the UK, people can go outside and even to the shops whenever the fuck they like. Even if it's for an emergency tin of corned beef.

But *everyone* seems to be going to the shops. Supplies of toilet roll are drastically declining for some reason. The constant news updates give Daddy mild panic attacks. Mummy takes it upon herself to source the family's toilet rolls and any other emergency supplies; primarily cheese and alcohol.

Follow the Piddleton family as they navigate their first ever lockdown and to see how they manage their overall toilet roll stock levels.

MEET DADDY PIDDLETON:

Daddy — or Percy to his friends — is currently locked down inside his house with his wife and two young daughters.

He's petrified of running out of toilet roll, but his is a long-standing fear. In 2006, he was on a road trip. Around the time his stomach started churning, he realised the coach he was travelling on didn't have any toilet roll. Percy came extremely close to soiling himself in front of his friend. And many strangers. Remarkably close.

To avoid a complete breakdown in the first days of lockdown, Percy limits his bowel movements to every other day.

There's already a new routine in place. Percy now divides his time between working from home, virtual workouts with Joe Wicks and home-schooling the kids.

On a normal day in the before times, Percy would put the measuring jug in the wrong cupboard without realising. The thought of ironing made his left eye twitch.

Percy goes to the fridge to check on the cheese reserves.

MEET MUMMY PIDDLETON:

Mummy's name is Pippa. She fancies Joe Wicks more than Percy. Joe Wicks is an online fitness guru. She sometimes looks at Joe for minutes on end before picturing Percy with a ponytail. Joe has incredible moves and lots of energy. Percy doesn't have either. Pippa loves the idea of working out at 9am after her Corn Flakes.

Pippa now works from home in a makeshift office next to her underwear drawer. It soon dawns on her that being stuck inside with Percy will become more annoying than ants.

Pippa has lots of ideas on how to home-school the eldest kid. She has accumulated more resources than the Department for Education.

Pippa won't head outside willy-nilly. She's the teacher's pet to Boris Johnson's headmaster. The rules are there to be followed to the tee. And rightly so.

Pippa dislikes *COVIDIOTS* more than Percy's worn out socks.

MEET PATSY PIDDLETON:

Patsy is the eldest of two annoying girls. Patsy has overheard Mummy and Daddy talking about the global pandemic and wonders when she will get to 'self-ice-skate'.

This summer, Patsy turns six years old. She's been planning her Frozen-themed party since her last birthday. Unfortunately, due to the entire planet coming to a standstill, Elsa and Olaf have been furloughed and are unlikely to resume partying any time soon. Patsy is patiently waiting for updates from the UK government about this.

Patsy has a younger sister. They argue a lot. Patsy hates her sister. Not all the time. Just when she's awake.

MEET PENELOPE PIDDLETON:
Penelope is named after a Thunderbird. She's the youngest. The infamous second child.

Penelope is overly aggressive, emotional and actively tries to maul her older sister. She's often mistaken for a wild hyena.

Penelope doesn't give a rat's arse about COVID-19. She only cares about her morning cereal being in the tiger bowl instead of the green one.

Nothing gets in Penelope's way. And if it does, she just punches and screams her way through it. And then bashes it around the head with a spoon.

Penelope is delightful.

WEEK 1:

LOCKDOWN BEGINS:

The first day of lockdown begins. Inside the tired-looking Piddleton home, there's an odd mix of enthusiasm and constant COVID-19 news bulletins. Pippa and Percy's enthusiasm drops when they hear how long lockdown might last.

They eat breakfast and drink some coffee. To motivate herself for the start of home-school, Patsy puts on her school uniform and freshly polished school shoes. Penelope, on the other hand, is still wearing her Weetabix-stained vest. But her hunger has been temporarily satisfied at least.

Patsy is aware something strange is going on because she now gets a biscuit at 8.55am. Normally, she would be at school doing phonics at this time.

Pippa is a social media lover. She suggests the family start each day with a workout. A Joe Wicks workout. Joe Wicks is an online global sensation, a perfect-looking specimen aimed at reminding parents that they have let themselves go over the years. He broadcasts from an immaculate room inside his house. The Piddletons' workout room — their living room — resembles a First World War trench.

THE PIDDLETONS IMMEDIATELY LOSE INTEREST IN
PE WITH JOE WICKS:

Percy, Pippa, Patsy and Penelope are enthusiastic for *PE with Joe Wicks* at first. Sweat pours from Percy's face. In fact, his sudden burst of energy petrifies the kids. They think his toilet-roll breakdown has finally kicked in.

But Percy thinks he might have found his true calling. He performs the Spiderman moves as if he were Peter Parker himself.

Reaching for the Stars is one of Percy's personal favourites. It gives him a private moment to remember long-lost dreams.

Pippa bails out mid-way through day 2. She's happy to watch. Percy realises that bunny-hopping around the living room on his own is more embarrassing than doing the workout in his pants.

Having retired from playing football a decade ago, Percy muscles ache for days. He initiates a Deep-Heat recovery programme to ease both the physical and psychological pain. Percy wonders why Joe Wicks' living room looks so happy.

Penelope gives Joe Wicks two workouts before demanding to watch Peppa Pig instead.

HOME-SCHOOLING AND WORKING FROM HOME BEGIN WITH INTENSE ENTHUSIASM: Patsy puts on her school uniform. She isn't going to school, though. She's going to the living room. Percy and Pippa excitedly take a photo. They're so excited to teach Patsy number bonds and keywords.

Patsy is utterly confused.

TOILET ROLL WORRY INCREASES:
In normal circumstances, Percy doesn't worry about toilet roll use. He goes about his toilet habits without a care in the world. Sometimes he even uses extra as a treat. But things have changed *quickly* during lockdown.

Try as he might, Percy can't figure out why people have decided to panic-buy toilet roll during a pandemic. If anything, it should be beer and cheese.

But now Percy is panicking. But not buying. He refuses to acknowledge toilet roll as the new gold dust. Percy has started having premonitions about wiping his arse with a tea-towel.

The family are down to their last toilet roll. Pippa decides to make curry for dinner.

Please pray for the Piddletons.

A PICTURE OF PIPPA WHEN PERCY RETURNS FROM THE SHOPS:

When Percy returns from the shops, he's greeted by what can only be described as the world's most dangerous cleaner.

Within a split second of opening the door, Pippa lunges toward Percy. She's got more gear than a Ghostbuster.

Percy can't enter until he has a Dettol hose-down and symptom check. He only popped out for bread and to look at butterflies.

But Pippa will do whatever it takes to stop the virus, even if it means suffocating her husband with anti-bac wipes and burying him in the back garden.

Once all checks are complete and Pippa is satisfied with Percy's health, he is granted temporary asylum. But he must self-isolate in the loft for 14 days.

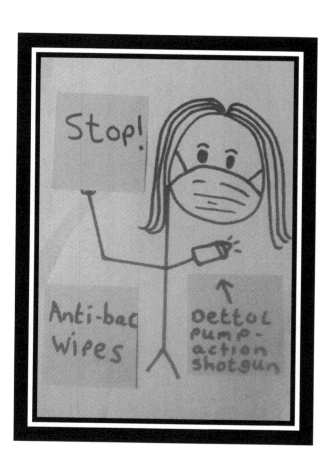

PANIC ON A SOCIALLY DISTANCED WALK: Percy is out on his government-permitted daily walk. The trouble is, so is everyone else. Percy sees potential virus carriers heading toward him on the exact same path. They're still over a mile away, but they might be asymptomatic.

Percy panics. He needs to divert *now*. But which way? He looks left and right but there's no obvious path to vacate to.

Percy and the surely diseased people get closer and closer. Almost half a mile now separates them. *SOMEBODY PLEASE DIVERT*.

Percy reacts before it's too late. He edges on to the grass verge. He's the hero the country needs.

PENELOPE HAS A SHIT DURING A WORK MEETING:

Penelope is a toddler. She has learnt how to verbally communicate. Talking is her new favourite pastime. She also likes to shit herself 2 or 3 times a day. Penelope also loves popping into Percy's home office unannounced to see him at work.

Percy is having an important meeting with senior management discussing ways to streamline a process. Penelope decides to show off her full skillset. She barges in on Percy's meeting and informs him that she has shit herself.

Percy's colleague sips on his coffee. He's glad he has no kids.

FLASHBACK FRIDAY:

Long before the pandemic, and prior to becoming a father, Percy Piddleton lived life on the edge. He did what he wanted when he wanted. He ran ultramarathons. He jumped from planes. He bungee jumped into canyons…naked.

Today, he recalled a walk he took through the Amazon rainforest 10 years ago. He felt at one with the incredible habitat. He saw some of the most intriguing animals he had ever seen.

He felt at one with the world.

The rain was warm and intense.

He was free.

Ten minutes ago, Percy walked to the Co-op to buy some paracetamol and a tin of baked beans. On the walk, he saw a dead tree, five vicious-looking dogs and some drunk men with their tops off.

It was raining. Pissing it down. Percy wasn't in a rainforest anymore.

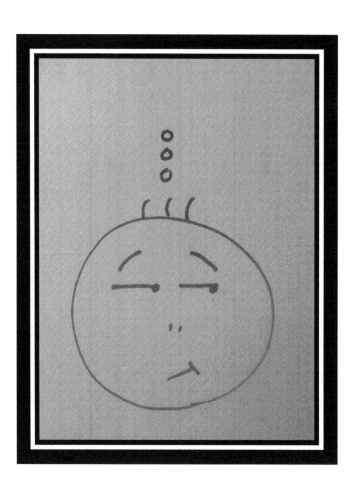

WEEKS 2 AND 3:

SOCIAL DISTANCING IN MARRIAGE:

Pippa and Percy have had an argument about whether shopping for jam is an essential trip outside. Percy loves jam on his toast. Pippa couldn't care less. Tensions rise. Pippa holds a concealed bottle of Dettol, her finger on the trigger.

Percy then annoys Pippa for the twenty-seventh time in three hours. But he doesn't know why. He thinks it's because he left the tea bag in her mug by mistake.

As a result, Pippa has decided to implement controversial social distancing guidelines.

Percy is not permitted within 10 metres of Pippa. She is also enforcing a face-like-thunder-until-Monday policy.

These harsh measures are nothing new for Percy. If anything, they suit him. It's the perfect opportunity to finally complete that game of Resident Evil he started in 2004.

NO ONLINE SHOPPING SLOTS FOR DECADES: Pippa can't get an online shopping slot until December 2044. Percy has been staring helplessly inside the fridge for 45 minutes. It's almost empty.

He has visited the fridge 246 times in a 24-hour period. The fridge is usually a loyal friend, but not anymore. Percy just wants a snack. Say, a Cornish Pasty. But the fridge offers nothing. It's barren. Like Percy's soul.

Percy considers going to *Co-Op*. But that requires Pippa dressing him up in a Power Loader from Aliens.

Percy is no Sigourney Weaver. He faces his stark reality and conjures a snack out of Mini-Babybels, rancid coleslaw and long-life milk.

PENELOPE ALMOST MURDERS PATSY AND PATSY BURNS PENELOPE'S TOYS:

Penelope is angry. So angry.

But this anger is different. It's new. This is coronavirus anger. It's the built-up frustration of looking at her older sister every hour of every day. Patsy insists on taking Penelope's toys from her. Standard sibling practice.

But Patsy has done this all week. All fucking week.

Penelope finally snaps in monumental fashion. She drags Patsy to the front door by the scruff of her neck, opens it and hurls her head-first into the recycling bin ready for the bi-weekly collection at 9am.

Patsy manages to escape. She staggers in through the open front window and snatches Penelope's toy keys from her. She burns them.

Pippa and Percy share a concerned look. Their daughters can now summon fire.

FUCK-ALL THURSDAYS:

Today is Thursday. The second Thursday of lockdown. A pattern is emerging with Thursdays for The Piddletons. Not a lot gets done. On *fuck-all Thursdays*, The Piddletons tend to stay in their pyjamas and forget to brush their teeth. They have breakfast at lunchtime. They have dinner at midnight. The kids snack whenever they bloody well like. By the time Thursday arrives Patsy and Penelope have morphed into Dickensian street urchins.

Pippa has called an emergency inset day on two consecutive Thursdays.

Other named days to in line for the home-school curriculum include, 'can't-be-arsed-with-Joe-Wicks-Mondays', 'we-all-need-sectioning-Tuesdays', and, 'let's-just-chuck-the-kids-in-front-of-the-tele-and-sit-in-separate-rooms-and-say-nothing-Wednesdays'.

WELCOME TO VIRTUAL WORLDS OF VIRTUALLY EVERYTHING VIRTUALLY IMAGINABLE:

Pippa is super-organised. It was her defining characteristic before COVID-19 struck. But during Lockdown, she has become an organisational oracle. Percy can't catch up.

Pippa's Instagram and Facebook feeds are full of wonderful ideas. During the first two weeks of home-schooling, Pippa has made everything humanly possible *virtual*.

Percy's favourite virtual world is the virtual farm. In this virtual world, he and the kids excitedly watch... sheep...eat...grass.

Percy now enjoys watching sheep eat grass more than eating posh cheese.

Pippa recommends a virtual family rave where the entire family dance around the living room as if they are in Cafe Del Mar in Ibiza. Minus the sunsets, copious alcohol and David Guetta, of course. And the feel-good vibe.

The kids aren't sure whether they now live in an alternative virtual reality parallel universe. Patsy has started talking about virtual poos.

PIPPA BRINGS CHRISTMAS TO EASTER:
Pippa follows various online lockdown groups. She has found two ideas for the Piddleton family Easter. Pippa is so happy.

It's the beginning of the Easter weekend. In the living room, Pippa and Percy are staring at a *fully decorated Christmas tree and a tent the size of a small town*. Percy is unable to get to the fridge in the kitchen and has called in the coastguard for assistance.

Pippa thinks she's at Glastonbury.

When the kids are in bed, Pippa and Percy get wasted in the tent while listening to Oasis on YouTube.

FLASHBACK FRIDAY:

Way before the pandemic, and prior to becoming a father, Percy Piddleton lived life on the edge. He did what he wanted when he wanted. He ran Ultramarathons. He jumped from planes. He bungee jumped into canyons...naked.

Today, he recalled all seven of his trips to Las Vegas at once. Ah, Las Vegas. Percy refers to it as his second home. It's a place where Percy lets his receding hair down by gambling the night away in luxurious casinos. It's a place to roam free, to look out into the desert and wonder how it's all possible. It's a place to go wild to international DJs in world-famous clubs.

It's a place to be young.

Today, Percy danced to Baby Shark seven times.

WEEK 4:

PIPPA REALISES SHE IS STUCK WITH PERCY: Pippa is annoyed with Percy. This is Pippa pictured three weeks into lockdown with him. It's official: a picture does tell a thousand words. These thousand words are exclusively about being annoyed at Percy.

Percy tries his best in life. He's laid back. Pippa is more Drill-Sergeant-during-basic-training-in-the-Marines type of laid back.

As far as lockdowns go, this isn't an ideal mix.

You see, Percy is obsessed with food. He is constantly thinking about it. He talks to himself about food. He repeatedly asks himself about the contents of his next meal.

He ponders whether, as a family, they should mix things up a bit by having dinner at lunch time.

Pippa doesn't give a monkey's toss.

Pippa arranges for the kids to do some colouring at the table. Percy interrupts and suggests he uses up some of the 301 eggs they have accumulated. Maybe he can fry some to put on their gammon this evening?

Has it been mentioned that Pippa is annoyed with Percy?

ALWAYS A TOWEL ON PIPPA'S HEAD:

Like millions of other people, Pippa has taken the executive decision to wear pyjamas every day. Gone are the days of getting dressed into daytime clothing and looking like a respectable human being. Pippa wears a very fetching pair of baggy, baked-bean stained red jogging bottoms. She teams these with a musky smelling large t-shirt. She hasn't washed it since lockdown started.

Pippa also appears to wear a towel on her head for at least 18 hours a day.

She wears it during her online work meetings for 400 people to see. She wears it when she bakes cakes with the kids. She wears it when she has a pop at Percy for moving the toaster three inches to the left.

Pippa loves the towel look. She finally blow-dries her hair seven minutes before going to bed before repeating the process the next day.

FAMILY ZOOM TIME:

Percy likes to check-in on his family during lockdown.

Trouble is, he can't hear a bloody word anyone is saying. In one ear, he has Patsy and Penelope physically and psychologically scarring each other. In the other ear, his mum rabbits on about the weather. But he can't see her because she doesn't know how to turn on her camera.

In another screen, his brother has his camera on but can't work the microphone. He's happy to remain silent throughout. There is also an extreme close-up of a niece staring at him strangely, like a scene from Paranormal Activity. The final screen shows his sister. Her cat enters the conversation and demands to be fed.

Percy's mum finally sorts herself out. He is greeted with half her head and a clear view up her left nostril.

FLASHBACK FRIDAY:

Way before the pandemic, and prior to becoming a father, Percy Piddleton lived life on the edge. He did what he wanted when he wanted. He ran Ultramarathons. He jumped from planes. He bungee jumped into canyons...naked.

Today, Percy recalled having a flying lesson in a plane. He was a bird. He was flying. He was free. The buzz was like nothing he had previously experienced. There was a moment during the lesson where he was given complete control of the plane. Percy could touch heaven.

Today, Percy took Patsy outside for her first lesson on her new bike. Patsy hated it. She ran away to the nearest church.

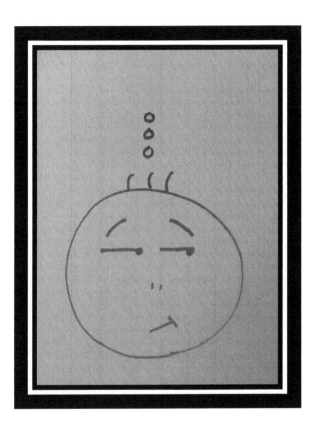

SATURDAY NIGHTS IN LOCKDOWN ARE WILD: Percy misses Ministry of Sound.

It's Saturday night. A week of home-schooling, working from home and worrying about whether there is enough cheese until the food shop arrives is being rewarded with a solo party in the garden.

Percy may be alone in the garden, but he is absolutely buzzing.

He is on his sixth beer. The sun is shining. The *Mamma Mia* soundtrack is playing. The kids are doing whatever they wish. Pippa is giving the door handles a good old anti-bac treatment.

Percy is loving life.

Unfortunately, it all gets too much for him. Within an hour he's asleep on the trampoline, naked.

Party
by
himself

NO MORE CHEESE IN THE FRIDGE:
As previously mentioned, Percy likes cheese. No. He *loves* cheese. He has single-handedly kept cows off the furlough scheme. But his love of cheese has moved on to the next level. It's now week three and Percy is days away from putting brie in his coffee. That is, if he had any.

Unfortunately, Percy has run out of cheese. And there's no imminent food delivery. He's forced to wait days on end for the milk and other essential produce to run low before he can justify an essential trip to Co-op.

This is music to Pippa's ears. With Percy staying at home, her anti-bac stock levels remain stable.

Percy feels lost. He sneaks out to the kitchen and starts pouring milk down the drain.

BREAKING NEWS: PIPPA SECURES TESCO DELIVERY SLOT:

After many long nights drawing up strategies to break the delivery-slot enigma, Pippa was tipped off by an unknown informer. They suggested that Tesco had released some additional delivery slots, but she had to move fast.

Quicker than you could say "Let's get some more eggs", Pippa threw Penelope on the sofa and sprinted to her laptop.

Slot secured. Food ordered. Pippa celebrates her achievement by hoovering the living room again.

WEEK 5:

WHEN THE KIDS OVERREACT TO ABSOLUTELY NOTHING:

This is Patsy and Penelope again. Lockdown is into the fourth week. Both girls have developed awfully close bonds with their plates and cutlery. If Pippa or Percy serve them a meal with any other plate or cutlery, Patsy and Penelope go utterly insane.

Patsy adopts a subtle approach. She accepts that plate-related mistakes happen. We're all human. But not the fork and knife. No. Never. How could Mummy and Daddy get this so wrong?

Patsy will whinge and mumble before walking into the kitchen and helping herself to the correct cutlery.

Penelope is a different kettle of fish. She's a second child. She adopts an aggressive, borderline violent approach. First, she stares at the plate with lifeless eyes. She needs to process the incomprehensible mistake made by Mummy or Daddy. She then refuses to eat. A mumbled rant follows. Screaming and crying follows that.

Penelope hurls the fully loaded plate into the neighbour's garden. They've got a rabbit out there. Or, at least, they did.

PERCY NEEDS AN URGENT POO:

A sudden twinge in the pit of his stomach means Percy needs a poo. It's urgent. Trouble is, Patsy and Penelope crave his attention all the time. Percy frantically holds his bowels while planning his escape to the toilet.

He doesn't know if he'll make it.

He panics.

He doesn't even know if they have enough toilet roll to cope with the anticipated load.

Percy makes a run for the stairs. Pippa is in the toilet. She has been in there for 45 minutes on her lunch break. She isn't having a poo or a wee. She's either meditating or posting a recent baking picture on Instagram.

Percy calls in the Armed Response Unit to knock the door down and drag Pippa away, so he can release his load.

HOME-SCHOOLING PRETTY MUCH CEASES TO CONTINUE:

Pippa and Percy can't be arsed to teach anymore. They're contemplating handing in their notice to the kids who are almost certain to accept.

It's not even teaching in the first place. It's just constant arguing and frustration at Patsy's refusal to engage in anything other than the snack cupboard.

Patsy doesn't even wear her school uniform anymore. Instead, she does phonics in her knickers. Penelope just wonders around the living room looking for an empty syringe for her next sugar fix.

Pippa and Percy will hold a briefing in due course.

PERCY KEEPS ON DRINKING:

Percy may have a problem. During these unprecedented times, his alcohol intake has risen to equally unprecedented levels.

During lockdown he has polished off two bottles of gin and pale ales from every country on Earth. He's even having a large sherry every night to help him sleep.

There's a rumour going around that Percy tried pouring a Smirnoff Ice on to his Corn Flakes. Unconfirmed reports also suggest that he's replaced his mid-morning coffee with a jug of Pimm's.

But Percy feels his alcohol intake has passed its peak and has begun to plateau. "I pour milk on my cereal like everyone else", he tweets. "We're all in this together".

Percy's phone shakes his hands. He can feel the second wave coming.

FLASHBACK FRIDAY:

Way before the pandemic, and prior to becoming a father, Percy Piddleton lived life on the edge. He did what he wanted when he wanted. He ran Ultramarathons. He jumped from planes. He bungee jumped into canyons...naked.

Daddy recalls the times when he and Pippa went out on spontaneous dates. No planning was required; just an urge to get up and go.

Percy and Pippa partook in leisure activities like getting shit-faced on Pimm's and Lemonade in beer gardens.

They enjoyed sharing jokes over exquisite meals in quaint restaurants. They used to have starters. Sometimes they even had pudding. They conversed eloquently between courses as if they had all the time in the world.

They sometimes kissed.

Today they ate beans on toast at lunchtime for the fifteenth consecutive lunchtime.

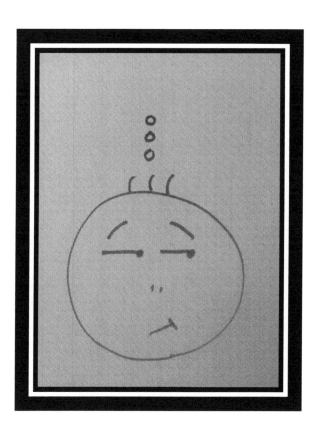

PERCY AND PIPPA ALWAYS ARGUE OVER GOVERNMENT GUIDELINES:

Patsy and Penelope are settled in bed. Percy and Pippa have some well-deserved downtime together. A date, if you will.

Within three minutes, the topic of conversation takes a turn for the worse. They talk about the latest government guidelines. It turns sour. They fall out. From out of the blue, Pippa proceeds to list fifty ways in which Percy annoys her.

Pippa storms upstairs and goes to bed. Percy grabs a biscuit and watches a repeat of the daily government briefing.

WEEKS 6 AND 7:

EASTER IS OVER AND HOME-SCHOOLING ARRANGEMENTS TENTATIVELY RESUME:

Patsy and Penelope have hit a wall. Engagement levels are at a record low. They're roaming around the house like cave people in search of their next kill.

Within an hour of resuming home-schooling, Percy suspends Patsy with immediate effect. No warnings. No meeting with the parents. No. He'd only be zooming with himself, anyway.

Percy asks Penelope to escort Patsy from the living room to her bedroom. Penelope wants a cereal bar as a reward.

Pippa and Percy debate the merits of opening a bottle of wine mid-morning. This quickly escalates to cashing in their multiple pensions so they can charter a private plane to Las Vegas. The casinos are empty, they saw it on the news. The alcohol, like them, is just sitting there waiting for something to happen.

Anything.

YES, LET'S HAVE INCREDIBLE FUN – LET'S PLAY VIRTUAL BINGO:

Percy and Pippa are in desperate need of a break from the kids, work, finding online shopping slots, hoovering and existence. Pippa loves ideas. She suggests playing a game of virtual bingo with her parents.

Pippa and Percy are pictured here showing their unbridled excitement at playing this intense game of numbers.

Percy thinks about his partying days in Ibiza. He didn't know what day of the week it was then, either. He smiles in the warm glow of comfort.

Pippa thinks about hoovering up the mess from the non-stop, alcohol-fuelled bingo extravaganza. But she's worried that the fun is too clean. She slides an open tube of Pringles to the edge of the table, behind Percy's elbow.

PERCY AND PIPPA ADMIT DEFEAT IN THEIR CONSTANT BATTLE AGAINST THE KIDS:

During their weekly press briefing, Percy and Pippa finally decided to step down as parents and let the kids run the house.

Their Chief Parenting Advisors calculated that the peak of Patsy and Penelope not listening to a word they say is, *months away* from flattening.

With snack requests at an all-time high too, the kids are simply not backing down. Percy and Pippa making preparations to spend the remainder of lockdown in the loft.

Following the briefing, Percy and Pippa shuffle around the house in their tired looking dressing gowns, their hair wild and unkempt. The kids, meanwhile, kick the living daylights out of each other over a box of Jaffa Cakes.

IT'S BLOODY RAINING AND PERCY IS CRYING: Six weeks into isolation and the heavens have opened. Walks are off the agenda. Even the garden is off limits. Percy starts panicking again. Mummy does the same. She's been holed up in the toilet for the past three hours.

Daddy is running out of ideas for kids' activities. It wasn't supposed to be like this. Tears trickle down his cheeks. He has done more baking than Mary Berry. He has read more princess books than Walt Disney. He has argued with a 5-year-old more times than he's had hot dinners. And to top it all off he's run out of beers, cheese and Jaffa Cakes.

Joe Wicks on catch-up it is then. Followed by a virtual tour of a farm to watch pigs eat mud.

PERCY REALISES HE IS TERRIBLY UNFIT: The Piddletons go for a walk through their local forest. When running away from the Gruffalo, Percy catches himself breathing a little heavily. Each step seems to take him closer to a heart attack. Percy also diagnoses himself with diabetes on the spot for good measure.

Unlike the Gruffalo, the lockdown baking has caught up with him. As his life flashes before his eyes, all he sees are cakes and biscuits.

Percy estimates that he has consumed more sugar in the past six weeks than he has in the previous three decades.

He has also eaten around 6 tonnes of cheese and washed that down with over 3,673 pints of ale — approximately.

When Penelope tells Percy that a monster troll is also chasing him, he passes out face down in the lake.

Percy now takes up a valuable bed in his local accident and emergency department.

He should have stayed at home.

95

FLASHBACK FRIDAY:

Way before the pandemic, and prior to becoming a mother, Pippa Piddleton lived life on the edge. She did what she wanted when she wanted. She got drunk Thursday to Saturday every week. She ended up on a drip in an Ibiza hospital. She flew helicopters in her spare time.

Today, Pippa recalls a shopping trip to New York over 10 years ago. Percy went with her, even though he isn't a fan of shopping. It was New York, after all. At worst, he'd have plenty of other things to moan about.

Pippa was delightfully content with browsing in the department stores. She had money to spend. A now foreign concept called *disposable income*.

She could spend without a second thought. And then spend some more for good measure.

Four gorgeous coats, two pairs of designer shoes and a $90 umbrella later, she went home satisfied.

Today, during five minutes of peace from home-working and home-schooling, Pippa brought some nappy bags, a set of teaspoons and some bin-liners on Amazon.

FRIDAY NIGHT VIRTUAL PARTY AND PIPPA GETS SMASHED ON THREE GLASSES OF WINE:

Pippa is normally a very sociable person. She has friends, even. Friday-night muscle memory kicks in and she decides to arrange a Zoom chat with some familiar faces.

Pippa sips on wine and laughs with her friends throughout the maximum two-hour Zoom slot.

Trouble is, Pippa doesn't drink much these days. By the second glass, she's well on her way. She has a peculiar grin when looking at Percy. He pulls the exact same face as he nears the end of his 16-year Resident Evil game.

By the third and final glass, Pippa is officially pissed. While Percy is sworn to secrecy, a household leak confirms that she was running around the street singing Tina Turner songs. When Percy rounded her up, she settled down with a Munch Bunch yoghurt and some garlic bread.

She then threw up in the kitchen sink. Pippa wonders what was so great about old Friday nights.

WEEKS 8 AND 9:

THE KIDS ARE BORED OF THE SAME DAILY WALK: Many weeks ago, the government gave the Piddletons permission to partake in daily exercise in their local area. Trouble is, they live in the most densely populated area of the solar system. There aren't many places to go without brushing shoulders with other human beings. For some reason, the other 27 billion people in his town want to go on a daily walk at the same bloody time. Most of these people never go on a walk, let alone a daily one.

After lunch, Percy tells the kids it's time for their daily walk. Predictably, they ignore him before continuing to thieve toys from one another.

HALF TERM IS HORRIFICALLY CLOSE: Pippa and Percy have suddenly realised that half term is fast approaching. Every day feels like a never-ending half term to them. The only difference between this type of half term and a home-schooling day is...well, there is no difference.

Patsy and Penelope still require a snack immediately after munching on their Shreddies. They still can't occupy themselves without causing utter mayhem. And they still barge in on Zoom meetings and tell Pippa's line manager that they just had a poo in the paddling pool.

Percy considers forging a document proclaiming he and Pippa are, in fact, keyworkers. This will get the kids out of the house for the week while they finally catch up with Tiger King.

'THAT' TIME OF THE WEEK AGAIN: It's Thursday in lockdown, which can only mean one thing for Percy: he decides to crack open some alcohol. Yes, Thursday appears to be the new Friday.

Percy has spent a worrying amount of hours thinking about how strange Thursdays are. He's drawn up several graphs. This was primarily to keep his mind off sweet, thirst-quenching, ice-cold beers Monday to Wednesday.

Not since the pre-kids-days of 2003 has Percy downed alcohol on a Thursday night. In now-demolished nightclubs, he would consume a town's worth of Vodka-Redbull for £17. All inclusive.

Apparently, they're banned now. Like seeing your family.

Percy counts: this is now seven consecutive Thursdays with alcohol consumption. That's lucky. Maybe he'll stop the run here.

He laughs. No. No, he won't.

PATSY'S HALF-HEARTED CLAPPING-FOR-CARERS CAUSES STREET RIOT:

Patsy isn't a confident clapper at the best of times. During the clap-for-carers weekly clap, a neighbour notes Patsy's lacklustre clapping. She decides to hurl abuse at Patsy.

More and more neighbours see Patsy's uninspiring clap. One neighbour lobs a dining room chair toward the Piddleton home. Another throws a Molotov cocktail.

Before you can say *we're all in this together*, a full-blown riot begins. The street is placed under military curfew.

A neighbour, who wishes to remain anonymous, said: "That ignorant little girl was goading us all. I've never seen such disrespectful clapping. She clearly hates the NHS and our nation. Lock her up".

YET ANOTHER WOODLAND WALK:
The Piddletons venture out on another woodland walk. They intend to use this allotted time to search for clarity; to find their true purpose in life.

Instead, Percy and Pippa shout at Patsy to stop pissing about with the Velcro on her sandals. In Patsy's mind, the Velcro comes unstuck.

It doesn't.

But Patsy spends the entire woodland walk bending down to re-attach the poxy Velcro 376 times.

Percy is now an expert in trees. He wishes he were a Tree Surgeon. Sometimes he even wishes he were an actual tree. Pippa loves the colours and the holly. She also loves almost fracturing her ankle on an unseen tree stump.

Penelope has now learnt to *not* walk. Pippa has to carry her for 10 miles. When they enter their street again Penelope asks to go in the pram.

When they return home, the only question Percy and Pippa have answered is if whether they still want to raise children.

WHAT CAN WE DO AGAIN?

The government have told the Piddletons to stay alert. But they aren't entirely sure what this means. They try some facial expressions, but they only land somewhere between utter confusion and bad hay fever.

The government have also permitted unlimited exercise. Pre-lockdown, Pippa and Percy only exercised when they walked to the pub. They got a taxi back.

Pippa and Percy aren't sure what else they can do.

Can they take their pet hamster out for a walk as long as other hamsters keep two metres away from theirs?

Can they stand in a field and scratch their arse if they are with other arse-scratchers from the same household?

Can they hop on their left foot to the nearest motorway and then jump up and down in the middle lane for 24 hours?

Nobody really knows.

Percy looks out the window. He struggles to fight a sudden urge to bum-shuffle to the nearest tree and give it a cuddle.

The Piddletons are finally going bonkers.

FLASHBACK FRIDAY:

Way before the pandemic, and prior to becoming a mother, Pippa Piddleton lived life on the edge. She did what she wanted when she wanted. She got drunk Thursday to Saturday every week. She ended up on a drip in an Ibiza hospital. She flew helicopters in her spare time.

Today, Pippa recalls her honeymoon with Percy in Dubai. They stayed in a luxurious resort in the middle of the desert. She remembers the private infinity pool directly outside their room. She remembers eating exquisite meals whilst overlooking the desert, its wildlife and overwhelming majesty.

Today, she put a tent up in the back garden. It overlooks a dirty fence and a row of terraced houses.

PERCY WANTS TO PLAY GOLF BUT ISN'T ALLOWED: The government have allowed garden centres and golf courses to re-open. Percy isn't a fan of compost, but he *is* a fan of hitting a small ball with a stick.

Percy needs to step outside into new environments. His brain has shrunk 45% since lockdown begun.

Pippa isn't keen on Percy going anywhere. She has seven unopened packets of anti-bac wipes to use before he even thinks about making drastic changes such as buying a putter and golf gloves.

Pippa appreciates his brain has shrunk. She's aware of his dwindling personality. But she's angry at his inability to understand that going to a golf course represents a huge infection risk.

On these vast, open fields, he could be only half a mile away from the nearest human — in fresh, less polluted air. In the gorgeous spring sunshine. Away from surfaces, doors, door handles, sneezing, coughing and bogeys.

The risk is too high in Pippa's eyes.

Instead of heading out to play golf, Percy sits on the toilet and has his third poo of the day. He picked up a tummy bug from snot on a door handle. Patsy placed it there on purpose.

WEEK 10 – HALF TERM:

THE CURIOUS CASE OF THE SOCIALLY DISTANCED PICNIC:

Boris Johnson recently told the Piddletons they could now *drive* to outdoor spaces. They could even relax in them. This includes having picnics with all the trimmings – as long as the Piddletons keep at least 1 light-year away from all other life forms.

Within 30 seconds of Percy tucking into his cheese and pickle sandwich, a group of dogs storm their picnic spot with one objective in mind – mayhem.

The dogs' owners are unapologetic. They enter the socially distanced picnic area to retrieve their feral animals, squashing the scotch eggs in the process.

A mere three minutes later, another T-rex of a dog ransacks what's left of the picnic. This time the owner claims the dog is deaf and blind and unable to hear any calls to stop. He then spends seven minutes running around trying to haul his dog away from the ravaged picnic.

A couple of elderly lovebirds then walk toward the Piddletons. They brush Pippa's chair with their swaying arms. Pippa is livid.

"The field is the size of Texas", she mutters under her socially distanced breath. "More importantly, it's fucking empty. Stay the fuck away".

121

VERY EARLY SOCIALLY DISTANCED TRIP TO THE BEACH:

5.00am. The Piddletons are awake. Percy drives them to a local beach for some much-needed sea air before the rest of the country descends upon it.

They park up, run around a bit and then drive back.

That's it.

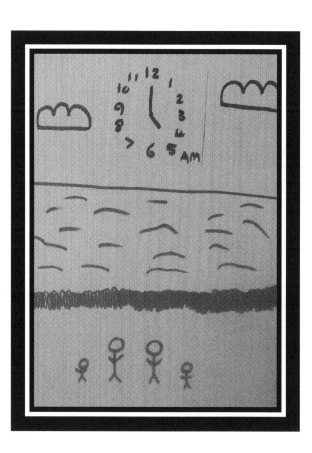

COURIERS LINE UP OUTSIDE THE PIDDLETON HOUSE

Pippa loves online shopping. She orders something new every day. But Pippa denies she has a problem.

Is it a problem when you have 37 separate deliveries per day? Not in Pippa's eyes. Every order is an essential item. Not to mention she's helping the economy.

Percy decides to look outside the bedroom window. He sees a queue of people in high-vis jackets snaking back from the front door, up the garden path and out onto the street.

Each person holds parcels of varying sizes. But they aren't family members dropping off birthday presents. They're DPD, Yodel and Amazon couriers. And if he's not mistaken, somebody from Uber Eats.

Maybe Pippa has ordered him a McDonald's?

No. It's a salad.

Pippa decides to put social-distancing markings on the garden path and a hand santiser dispenser by the front door.

TESCO SLOTS SOURCED FOR THE REMAINDER OF PIPPA'S LIFE

Pippa manages to secure online shopping slots until her approximate year of death. She books a few extra beyond that and leaves them to Patsy and Penelope in her will.

Percy can't wait to try every single type of ice-lolly until he's placed in a care home.

FLASHBACK FRIDAY:

Way before the pandemic, and prior to becoming parents, Pippa and Percy Piddleton lived life on the edge. They did what they wanted when they wanted. They sailed the Atlantic Ocean. They climbed vertical cliff faces. They hiked the entire Sahara Desert.

Today, Pippa and Percy recall the time they met whilst on a gap-year expedition to the Galapagos Islands. In this awe-inspiring setting, they immediately fell in love with each other. So much so, they got hitched on those very islands surrounded by the native turtles.

Today, in their back garden, they found a dead pigeon in the soil during a forest school lesson with Patsy.

WEEKS 11 AND 12:

HOME-SCHOOLING FADES IN TO OBLIVION (AGAIN):

Unfortunately, due to unforeseen circumstances related to complete lack of motivation, Pippa and Percy have ceased all home-schooling operations again. They have decided to furlough themselves indefinitely.

Patsy and Penelope are not kids of keyworkers, so they can just do whatever the fuck they like until they move out.

Percy and Pippa burn laptops, books, pens, felt-tips, paper and all other school resources on a huge bonfire in the back garden.

They kiss with a long-lost passion.

Home-school is closed. Done. Finished. Caput.

PIPPA FORCES PATSY TO GO BACK TO SCHOOL ON HER BOTTOM:

Lockdown is nearly over. Children can go back to school and grown-ups can go back to work. Government guidelines state, however, that people should avoid public transport, cars, bikes, walking (including crab-walking), running, skipping, skateboarding and camel riding.

But Pippa is one step ahead of the crowd. She forces Patsy to bum-shuffle all the way to school. At the moment, Patsy doesn't realise she lives a mile from her classroom door.

"There's nothing in the rules saying they aren't allowed to shuffle on their bum", Pippa says on her Facebook account.

An air ambulance touches down in the school playground. The paramedics take Patsy to hospital for third-degree burns on both bum cheeks.

PIPPA AND PERCY HEAD BACK TO WORK FOR A REST:

Pippa and Percy's working lives have changed so much during lockdown. The biggest change of all is working without physically being at work.

The trouble is, they really need to head back because their sense of humour has all but disappeared. Taking on board the government guidance on travel, they decide to use the newly discovered black hole in their garden to travel between their workplaces, home and the recently re-opened McDonald's.

Percy went back to work on Monday and has not been seen or heard from since. Pippa needs to get home for a quick hoover before the Tesco delivery person arrives.

SOCIALLY DISTANCED SCHOOLS REVEALED: Patsy is having a great time at school. She has a new normal. To abide by strict government guidelines on social distancing, each child must stay away from all other children until they are adults.

All pupils have been given their own personal classroom and a single chair to sit on. All previously used educational and play-related materials have been burnt or taken to the tip for safe disposal.

Patsy's classroom is fully COVID-secure. It has been painted white and the windows have been boarded up. She's only allowed to go to the toilet when her teacher tells her to.

At lunchtime, Patsy isn't allowed outside her classroom and must only eat plain paper. To drink, she is encouraged to catch her sweat droplets with her tongue.

Patsy is permitted to walk around the class with her hands behind her back, blindfolded, before returning to her chair. She then spends the remainder of the school day learning how to escape from hostage situations.

139

TEACHERS WEAR ASTRONAUT SUITS FOR PROTECTION FROM KIDS:

School is back. Teaching is evolving. All returning children are assumed to have COVID-19 until proven otherwise. As a result, Patsy's teacher takes no chances and wears a fully functioning spacesuit developed by NASA.

The UK government are procuring oxygen away from NHS hospitals to give to schools so teachers can breathe whilst wearing the state-of-the-suits.

TEACHERS SMOKE AND SIP ON PROSECCO DURING LESSONS:

Teachers at Patsy's school are so bored due to lack of children returning that they've taken up smoking and getting wasted during lessons.

Patsy tells Percy that her teacher held an illegal classroom rave during her literacy lesson today. When she asked about her education, the teacher told her to stop being such a nerd.

Some children at Patsy's school are over four times the recommended blood-sugar level. They've been given unlimited access to the Haribo sweet cupboard usually reserved for naughty children.

Patsy's Teaching Assistant has also been seen popping out to the local off licence to buy prosecco and Pringles for Maths.

PENELOPE IS TAKEN BACK IN TO COVID-SECURE NURSERY BY CARRIER PIGEON

In a further sign of returning normality, Pippa and Percy decide to send Penelope back to nursery. Not because it's 100% safe from the virus, or for her to increase her social skills and overall life chances.

Pippa and Percy are simply at their wit's end. They are falling apart at the seams.

New requirements mean that parents can't come within two miles of the premises. Effectively an ASBO.

Pippa uses her initiative by ordering a carrier pigeon from Amazon. Patricia the pigeon safely transports Penelope for her first day back at nursery by releasing her at the 'drop-off' point on the nursery roof.

Penelope catches a cold by lunchtime and is sent home for a year.

FLASHBACK FRIDAY:

Way before the pandemic, and prior to becoming parents, Pippa and Percy Piddleton lived life on the edge. They did what they wanted when they wanted. They sailed the Atlantic Ocean. They climbed vertical cliff faces. They hiked the entire Sahara Desert.

Today, Pippa and Percy recall a time when they were not tired. A time where they could breathe without their eyes falling out. Where they could sleep for eight uninterrupted hours. Where their heads felt like they were attached to their bodies.

This morning, Pippa and Percy were woken up at 4.58am by Penelope. She demanded breakfast immediately. Percy and Pippa haven't received any REM sleep since the night before Patsy was born.

WEEK 13:

SCRUFFY PIPPA BOOKS A SEAT ON ELON MUSK'S ROCKET TO GET AWAY FROM IT ALL:

Pippa is flaking out. She has had enough of lockdown. Her hair looks like days-old candyfloss. Her clothes look burnt. Her soul slowly darkens. She needs to get away from civilisation.

The UK government has eased restrictions on space travel. Pippa pounces on this by booking herself on to one of Elon Musk's SpaceX spaceships to travel to the International Space Station.

She maxes out all her credit cards, re-mortgages the home and sells the kids to fund the trip.

Pippa safely lands on the Space Station to begin six peaceful months of self-isolation.

She considers a trip to Mars if a second wave becomes a reality.

151

PEOPLE QUEUE UP OUTSIDE PRIMARK TO BUY PANTS AND SOCKS:

Non-essential shops have re-opened. Percy has holes in his pants and socks, but Pippa sees these items as non-essential items. Therefore, Percy is not authorised to join any queue whatsoever. He will continue to wear underwear that skirts the line between solid and gas.

Or he can just order online.

But Percy must continue to work from his bedroom, home-school a wild vampire and entertain a small crocodile. He has no time for underwear shopping.

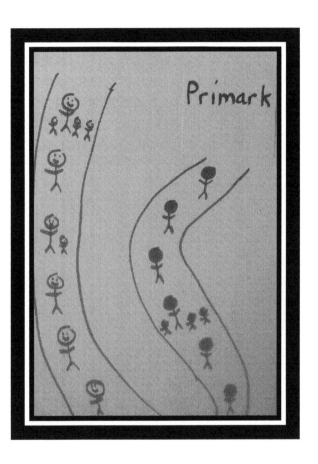

MCDONALD'S RE-OPENS BUT ONLY SELLS
PACKED FRUIT:

The British public eagerly queue for hundreds of miles outside recently opened McDonald's restaurants. Due to staff levels and social distancing measures, a reduced menu is advertised. Only packed fruit is on offer. Today is 'Melon Monday's'. The British public still queue. The British public love a queue.

FLASHBACK FRIDAY:

Way before the pandemic, and prior to becoming parents, Pippa and Percy Piddleton lived life on the edge. They did what they wanted when they wanted. They sailed the Atlantic Ocean. They climbed vertical cliff faces. They hiked the entire Sahara Desert.

Today, Pippa and Percy put Patsy and Penelope in the loft and watched Netflix all day.

PIPPA AND PERCY'S MOTIVATION LEVELS
DISAPPEAR TO UNKNOWN PLACE AGAIN:
Today is tough for Percy and Pippa. Their energy levels and enthusiasm for home working, home-schooling and, well, home-entertainment diminished weeks ago.

Today, their motivation to do absolutely anything has gone. Completely and utterly disappeared. They want to stay in bed and look at the ceiling. They have no interest in being a parent, no motivation to make breakfast. They can't be arsed to hoover and have no interest in going through phonics keywords with Patsy.

Pippa and Percy spend the remainder of the day looking out of their bedroom window at the opposite row of terraced houses.

FINAL WEEKS:

PATSY HEADS TO SCHOOL FOR LUNCH:

Patsy bum-shuffles back to school for her reduced-hours education. This week, Patsy is only permitted to attend at lunch times. Patsy loves lunch. Patsy eats her government-funded hot lunch and hails a taxi to return her home just in time to watch Waffle the Wonder Dog until dinner time.

Patsy is now off school for her six weeks summer holidays.

PIPPA NOW WORKS OUT 24-HOURS A DAY

Pippa has been virtually working out for the duration of lockdown. Just not consistently.

But she's stepped it up a level. She now works out pretty much every minute of the day.

Wherever Percy is in the house, he sees Pippa thrusting her arse in the air. It's as if Pippa has been possessed by a fitness demon. She shakes violently, shedding the lockdown biscuit crumbs staining her soul.

Whenever Percy enters a room, he checks the walls and ceilings first. He's certain he'll find Pippa crawling on all fours with her head twisted the wrong way.

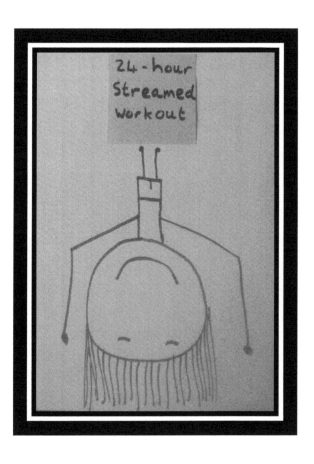

LOCKDOWN IS ALMOST OVER: PIPPA AND PERCY GO TO THE PUB ON THEIR FIRST DATE SINCE GLOBAL CLOSURE:

The 'new normal' has arrived. A socially distanced visit to the pub is here. Not since before their government told them to stay at home have Pippa and Percy enjoyed any time to themselves.

A 15-minute slot to visit the pub is booked online via the recently implemented Public Health England Public House app. Only two customers are allowed inside a pub per day, but they can drink as much as they bloody well like within those 15 minutes.

Pubs are then closed for a week to deep-clean the piss and vomit off the floors and walls.

Patsy and Penelope need a babysitter. And socially distanced babysitting is the new normal. To save on petrol and effort, their grandparents babysit them via Microsoft Teams.

During their 15-minute bender, Pippa and Percy roll back the years by getting shit-faced on jugs of Blue Lagoon, Tequila Sunrise and Sex on the Beach. They are chucked out of the pub after 10 minutes.

Lockdown is over and their new lives have begun.

IT'S HOLIDAY TIME

The world is now open. Humans can travel freely again. And most importantly, kids can stay with their grandparents.

Pippa and Percy are the first people in the world to book a holiday. Only this is not an ordinary holiday. Pippa and Percy have decided to take a gap year...by themselves. Patsy and Penelope are going to stay with their grandparents for twelve months.

Pippa and Percy are knackered. They just want to spend the year rekindling their love, restarting their souls. They want to have a shit in peace.

They aren't wasting any time. They are flying out tomorrow. To support local businesses, they have booked the kids a taxi to get to their grandparents' house. It's this type of selfless decision that will help get their country moving again.

LOCKDOWN IS OVER:

So, there you have it. After 15 weeks of being holed up in an underground bunker, the Piddletons are allowed back out into the big wide world. They can hike through those dangerous deserts, they can jump out of those planes, they can sail the seven seas.

No, they can't.

Unfortunately, the virus has not disappeared. The world has got to wait for a vaccine. In the meantime, the Piddletons have got to learn to live with the virus around them.

Kind of like how Pippa is forced to live with Percy forgetting to close cupboards.

Or on a par with Percy learning to live with Pippa's insistence on adding spinach and kale to the food shop.

Or Penelope learning to live with Patsy's borderline Satanic tendencies.

Or how Patsy is learning to live with being a second child and her subsequent unimportance.

From the depleted souls of the Piddletons exiting lockdown, they wish you all the best.

Stay distant. Bum-shuffle to school. Do not stockpile toilet roll.

FYI – Total Parcels delivered during lockdown: 3,648.

ACKNOWLEDGEMENTS:

I would like to thank Neil Roberts of NICW Illustrations for designing and creating the front cover. A huge thanks also goes to Robert Stimpson for editing.

I would also like to thank my parents for the genes to enable me to draw such awful (but funny) drawings.

And finally, I would like to thank my two daughters and my wife for providing me with the material to create this rather exaggerated account of these truly unprecedented times of 2020.